The symbolism of the inverted satanic cross represents the abuse and con of western civilization by the current and past dictatorships. Whilst this dictatorship remains then democracy is turned on its head. Once the populace recognises this state of affairs, it can turn the cross right side up, giving us back our lost freedom. The symbolism of the drops of blood is the upset, pain, anguish and sometimes the devastation of individuals and their families lives. These are imposed on the British people, by its politicians and the arms of government, along with the murder and ruination of millions due to an aggressive and psychopathic British foreign policy.

The symbolism of the flames represents the power and energy in a political system. When inverted, there is an attempt to deny the laws of nature. But that cannot last for too long before the flames will set light to the cross and the whole of society will burn and self destruct. Respect for the laws of nature, respecting people s human nature, their instincts and the urge for freedom and personal responsibility. By giving them rule over their own lives. Giving them the right to choose and not to be manipulated and dictated to. Thereby turning the cross upright to its natural position so that the flames may burn as the laws of nature and of physics intended.

DEMOCRACY: THE CON OF THE CENTURY

G.M. Solon

authorHOUSE®

AuthorHouse™
1663 Liberty Drive
Bloomington, IN 47403
www.authorhouse.com
Phone: 1-800-839-8640

Published by AuthorHouse   11/09/2012

ISBN: 978-1-4772-3145-6 (sc)
ISBN: 978-1-4772-3146-3 (e)

Dedicated to

Those who want the Freedom to choose,

And not to be wilfully abused.

Thanks to

My wife and son for typing and proof reading the manuscript. For also having to endure the trials and tribulation that led to the realisations in this book.

Table of Contents

Introduction

The essence of this book is in the first two chapters: what Democracy is, and that we don't have it.

It could have been left there for readers, by thinking for themselves, to discover the rest. The rest of, and bulk, of the book explains the tyrannies that are and have gone on. Tyrannies are large—such as the Invasion of Iraq—and small 'pestering, fine deceits, such as the confused signage on parking plates. I have included a range of abuses.

To my knowledge there have only ever been two real democracies in our world: the original, in ancient Greece c500BC, set up by Solon; and the other in Switzerland set up about 150 years ago and is on-going. By looking at Switzerland, one can judge what is and is not working in practice. What jumps out there is Corporate influence. This is not surprising, as Corporatism did not really exist at the inception of democracy in Switzerland, but has crept up on it. This brings us to some of the shortcomings of this book.

All political systems are culturally, philosophically and morally based, and whilst this book crosses over these issues, it does not discuss them per se. Democracy is a practical system to prevent tyrannies. However, what a tyranny is, is not always obvious.

Further shortcomings of this book, as well as of any fixed systems, arise from the three major factors that apply to almost any real world measure: PEOPLE, PLACE & TIME, with cultural background/ethos coming in on their coat tails. Any political system must have the flexibility to adjust to the above 3 factors. If we look to America's political founding fathers we see that they were well aware of how politics can become corrupt; so they set up the "Bill of Rights" to protect against it. But it strikes me that the Bill of Rights is an almost out of touch and defunct document today.

This book does not address how a country adopts the essential principles of People Power and accountability, or how to elaborate on these principles to suit its society. Setting up a Democratic system is not touched upon in this book, only some of the problems to overcome and a system that protects against tyranny are dealt with.

This book is short, as are the chapters, so the message does not get lost under data. To argue every issue that is raised is an encyclopaedic work. Your intuition and thinking powers can take you there. Where there is affirmation there is negation; in other words, there is no end to argument. One can not live life on that basis of intellect alone and this book is not written on that basis alone either.

At the risk of being repetitive, but due to a concern that the essence of this book will be lost under the mass of words: the first two chapters, whilst basic, are all important.

I would ask one more indulgence of the reader. Please look for the meaning behind my words, or, as one of our greatest linguistic philosophers, Bertrand Russell, put it, 'words are transparencies'.

G.M. Solon
Cambridgeshire 2012-03-21

PART I

Folly

Every day we are told we live in a democracy. We have been told it by our parents, our siblings, our peers, our grandparents, our teachers, our politicians. The BBC website declares "Democracy in Action". All the news channels repeat it in some report or other every day. Books argue its wonderments and numerous universities have courses containing large programmes on it.

There is just one problem: WE DO NOT HAVE DEMOCRACY. What we have in Britain[1] is Representative Government and that is something very, very different.

---

[1]   As in most Western Governments, excluding Switzerland

What is Democracy?

We need to take a look at its origin with the Ancient Greeks who had been under the domination of one tyrant after the other, who had stolen their wealth and oppressed the populace, time after time. Needless to say, they were fed up. Eventually a group of noblemen got together and arranged the problems along with some solutions, and then gave the task to a man called Solon to devise a short monograph on the matter of how to prevent more tyrannies by new rulers.

What Solon came up with to prevent tyrannies had two main components: 1. Have as many people as possible voting on the main issues that ruled their society; 2. Make those people appointed into positions of authority accountable for their actions. These two components are what I refer to later as the Essence of Democracy.

In practice this was restricted. The cultural set-up put inhibitors on these principles. Women and non-householders were omitted mainly because they were uneducated, although there were other prejudices reinforcing the exclusion of these two groups. It is easy to mix up the Essence of Democracy with cultural matters, but it is important to distinguish the two. In our current system of 'Representative Government' we did not give votes to women until 1928; it did not mean we did not have Representative Government, it just meant it was diluted.

To put ancient Greece into perspective, let's look at some cultural practices going on at the time. For instance, the Priests of Dionysus, at one of their festivals, would come out brandishing their swords and, if any women did not run away, they were cut down where they stood. Because Democracy is in place does not mean Justice is a given or tyrannies cannot arise. Laws and management must also be developed. Other developments which were decided, such as a law for national holidays for temple worship, were posted outside the relevant place i.e. on the temple in this case. These secondary issues of culture will not concern us. We will focus on the two main issues (Essence) of 'mass voting', and 'accountability' of those in positions of authority.

Shortly after Solon drew up his plan it was popularly called 'democracy'. Democracy is the current English word, derived from the Ancient Greek *demos* ($\delta\tilde{\eta}\mu o\varsigma$) meaning people, and *kratos* ($\kappa\rho\acute{\alpha}\tau o\varsigma$) meaning power, although a direct translation of *kratos* is rule/might. Nevertheless the most apt translation is 'PEOPLE POWER'.

People Power is the key to preventing Tyranny; that is, the people hold the power by being able to vote on any issue of the State, and especially over those appointed to positions of authority.

Let us now look at ,in PART II, what is wrong with the existing system and the Tyrannies that arise in it.

PART II

Word Abuse and Statistics

When you are being conned, you can bet that the con artist is telling you things that you think mean one thing but that he actually holds to mean something different.

The government's definition, for example, of the word 'homeless' does not mean you are homeless. It means, for instance, there are two people sharing a room. "Why do they do it?" you ask. Because they can then fiddle the figures to make it look like we require more housing. In the 1990s, when countries like Poland became EU members, there was an influx of over 1 million immigrants from Poland into Britain. They all found accommodation. If there had been a housing shortage, as the government claimed at the time, then none of them would have found accommodation. Recently, in a House of Commons debate, it was announced that 1 million affordable homes were vacant, but still institutions are claiming housing shortages with bogus statistics as if these statistics were genuine.

But why do they want these false statistics? If you investigate, you will find that the more houses there are, the more council tax they can collect, property developers want an expanding market as do housing associations, and everybody wants a bigger better (at a lower price) house. The big wish, however, is coming from overseas, where every third world bod wants the easy touch English to provide them with a lovely home and the life style that comes with it i.e. social security payments. Much better than a Bedouin tent or a corrugated iron shack with under-nourishing food and scarce water. Many immigrants are not from the third world but from the European Union, and they come because their life style is poorer at home and the opportunities this country offers are better. Thus the **desire** for more housing is enormous. The power to implement more house building rests with some of our major institutions, who use the false statistics as the justification for the new building. The new housing may be taken up by existing British citizens, but what they vacate is taken up by immigrants. However, the vast majority of the indigenous population do not want this expansion because it increases our overpopulation and the acute problems that overpopulation causes. Of course, more housing and infrastructure is defacing and diminishing the countryside, which is now overly encroached upon.

Let's look at an example of the current use of the word democracy being used as a lie and why that is so. If it has not yet become obvious it soon will.

Take Professor Dahl of Yale University in his book 'Democracy'. He defines Democracy as People Rule. '*kratos*' cannot just be translated as 'rule'. What appears as a small change in meaning is actually a large change in meaning, as you can see if you read his book and how he upholds America's Republic as a democracy.

I don't think John Harvard[2], an ancient Greek linguist and classicist, to which the founder of Yale University owed his education, would be very impressed.

"Abuse the word, con the People".

---

[2]   Founder of Harvard University

Deception by Politicians

The practice, not just of word abuse, but wholesale deception, is common in politics and government today. Politicians are well known for their deceit as well as their outright lying. We could leave matters here but some examples and explanations are in order.

Politicians can lie as much as they like (in Britain) with impunity; that is they are unaccountable or cannot be punished for lying. Even in an extreme case as Tony Blair (ex Prime Minister) going to Parliament and stating to the whole country that Iraq had weapons of mass destruction and was thus declaring war on Iraq, thereby deceiving the 650 MPs and the whole British population, he got away with the lie.

An interesting documentary was put on TV where the journalist made up a mock white paper, which was in essence to prevent MPs from lying, and to punish them for doing so. He gave the document to Jack Straw, a Member of Parliament and Cabinet Minister, asking him to adopt it and put it forward to the House. Jack Straw laughed at the document and the journalist. For Jack Straw, democracy is a joke.

The arrays of deceptions go on and on, from false promises before elections to non-implementation of promises after elections. Doctored statistics make things look good. The implementation of hidden government agendas are never mentioned publicly. Politicians are regularly imprisoned for fraud and contempt of court. They have also fiddled their expenses but that is alright because they responded "now we are caught, we will give the money back". Then there are the million pound annual consultancy salaries of banks to Blair and Mandelson. Must be legitimate though old chap, a what? The deceptions are so numerous you can all find your own examples of politicians' immorality.

One Vote Every Five Years

Our voting system allows you one vote every five years. Sorry, you also get a vote for your District and County councillor. This hardly constitutes People Power. Just the opposite. What it shows is how much power people do *not* have. To have democracy, people should be able to vote on all the issues concerning the management of the country and the making of its rules and laws. We have *none* of this.

Our one vote is for one Member of Parliament, who will supposedly do everything that we wish him to do to represent us. Sounds impossible? That is because it is. Not only does our MP represent us, he represents another 100,000 people[3]. Were a Member of Parliament to spend 6 minutes on one issue per person, he would need to work more than 24 hours a day for the whole year. The MP would have no time to eat his meals, sleep or go to the toilet and the year would still need to have in it another 1,000+ hours. Of course there is not one issue per person but thousands.

---

[3] This approximation is derived using round numbers i.e. 60,000,000 UK population between 650 MPs.

"What do they do then?" is the obvious question.

If you have ever contacted your MP, you probably got a diplomatic fob off: a standard letter with your name and address punched in, along with some personalised details, but which actually amounted to nothing much. MPs rely on the nanny state, the enormity of your ignorance, propaganda, more government department fob offs to CONTROL people, which is the key concept. They are given 3 minutes to consider if a Statutory Instrument (the final legal document when a law is enacted) should be passed. Yes that's three minutes.

The next chapter deals with what happens if you get passed first base and your letter gets dealt with.

Member of Parliament Competence

Question: how many Conservatives does it take to change a light bulb?

Opposite where I live, they cut down an orchard and built an affordable housing scheme, despite promises by Bayer Chemicals, who previously owned the land, that the orchard would remain as a shield to the village from their chemical and genetic testing. Once built, a 1m high light was erected on the road verge. This light was causing glare at night, and was easily mistaken for a motor bike or road vehicle. It was, in essence, causing a traffic accident risk. As none of the Parish Council, District Council or the Housing Association were prepared to do anything, we wrote to our local MP. We asked if we could get the light bulb changed or have the lamp post have a baffle put on it. He was very obliging, and, about 24 letters on, he gave up. The light still remains a danger. A changed bulb would cost about £5.00. The MP's name? Andrew Lansley. He is now the Secretary of State for Health.

Answer: It takes more than one Cabinet Minister and his support staff.

Is this really surprising? Not that surprising when you realise that MPs are all amateurs at the jobs they do. Yet, they head the various government departments and are directing what is done from an extreme level of ignorance. Not only that but they seem intent on maximising the level of inability of the Minister in a post e.g. Liam Fox is a Medical Doctor but was appointed Minister for Defence.

What skills do politicians have? Well, the main one is rhetoric which is also known as humbug. On account of rhetoric often uses the fallacy of logic. MPs are amateurs using the fallacies of logic to head the main departments that manage the country. A recipe for disaster.

Current Voting Choice

It does not matter which party you vote for, the Government gets in. A common enough phrase used by the Intelligentsia to the Labourer.

It is not that surprising that the above inference is taken. After all, the country faces the same problems whoever gets in, and the solution choices are limited, so when the civil services are put into action, the same old things happen with a fresh spin put on them by the new government's propaganda department. To be fair, there are some differences in party policies and these will produce some different results. If we look at our voting choice it can be seen that the bulk on offer is the same with the differences highlighted in election times and this makes it look like we have a choice.

There are 3 main parties, but the competition is between only 2 parties: Labour and the Conservatives with the Liberal Democrats coming in on the coat tails of the other 2. Is this choice? Hell is it. It is Hobson's choice.

Parties market themselves as all things to all men because they can maximise their vote that way. Most elections are won by winning over minority groups such as the handicapped and promising them this and that. This has led to the view that political parties are buying votes. The other major election-winning aspect is the marketing and advertising/propaganda campaign. This requires huge amounts of money so that campaigning can be done on a national level. This is why so few people or groups can mount a real election drive and the eligible parties are few in number.

The existing system recognises only that you vote for an individual and not because he is a member of a particular party. What actually happens is usually the reverse: the candidate is ignored and the party he represents is what is voted for. Voters are the victims of party politics, with a system whose propaganda over long periods of time has convinced people to vote for a party not for an individual.

Let's take a quick look at what happens when these MPs and Parties get into power. They initially do a number of good works as promised but these decrease with time. Then there is their hidden agenda that no one else is told about except their own members. If these are Bills, they are presented and pushed through the House quickly or they may be hidden within the national security cloak. The majority of the country's management issues, that only the relevant civil service have knowledge of, are never known about publicly except when a civil servant occasionally blows the whistle and then the public does get to hear about it. The Freedom of Information Act seems to have had little effect except to make the life of journalists easier.

You might disregard all of what has just been said on the basis that what happens at many general elections is that people are sick of the party in power so they vote against them so as to get them out. Still this does not improve our lot for long because the new party becomes the one we are sick of and we vote them out ; then the cycle comes round again.

Our politicians' skills are with 'rhetoric' and not much else. It is therefore not surprising that they make a complete hash of running the country, relying on excuses and clever phrases to get by. Let's face it, they are just incompetent. Please apply your own examples. I don't doubt that they are numerous.

What we require is to vote into jobs and office the individuals with the key skills to do a specific government job, in combination with dealing with the public and its institutions. This cannot be done under the present system. Instead we have self-perpetuating cliques employing their own.

Summary: In theory, the system allows anyone to become an MP. In reality you have 3 choices of Party, the third, the Liberal Democrats, having limited scope. Most voters have never read the parties'

Manifesto and know equally as little about the person (prospective MP) they are voting for. Even if you have informed yourself of the last two points, you have little idea and no control of what MPs or parties do once they are elected. To add to this, they are poorly qualified for the job they do and as consequence make a hash of the country's governance.

Something is seriously wrong, and you and I can do nothing about it. Please do not say you will write to your MP or vote for John instead of Fred in 5 years' time. Only changing the political system to Real Democracy will bring the necessary changes and prevent the Tyrannies.

Learned Helplessness

The Russian psychologist Pavlov, famous for his experiments with salivating dogs, discovered a phenomenon of great importance when his labs were accidentally flooded and he observed his dogs no longer responded to danger stimuli. They just lay there submissively, waiting for the inevitable danger to wreak its consequences. Further research has been extended to human behaviour and this phenomenon has been labelled as 'learned helplessness'.

It should be obvious if you extend this to social engineering and continuously frustrate people into getting nowhere with their petitioning against the state that they will give up and not bother.

Are governments about controlling people? The answer should again be obvious. Control, for dictatorships, is necessary and advantageous. The issue should be: is what is being done advantageous to society and is it done with our consent or is it being done subversively or idiosyncratically?

We have already looked at the power of our say and of our control. We get one vote in five years and fobbed off letters from our MP. So government is not done with our direct consent. Makings laws is the major means of control, at least in the sector of government control we are aware of. Not only are we not aware of the thousands of laws that are made, we know even less as to what these laws mean, their detail, how they are to be interpreted, and how we are supposed to comply with them.

I'll come back to the legal system later. For now, we will continue with subversive control and government threats of violent control.

"Pay your Tax or we will crush your car". Yes, it was a Labour party TV ad designed to bash you into submission.

"You have until the end of the month to submit your Tax Return". Then more quietly stated elsewhere: "If you fail to mention any earnings you will be imprisoned for tax evasion". That is, if you don't give us your hard earned income voluntarily we will persecute you with physical violence if necessary and/or incarceration, and you will pay the financial costs for the privilege of it. The government will take your money by force and do with it whatever they fancy without your consent e.g. to help kill tens of thousands of people in Iraq.

In normal language taking money against your will is knows as theft. Using it then to kill people is known as premeditated murder. This is what your government is doing, theft and murder.

There are people who believe in taking your money and redistributing to those less well off, either by direct hand outs or by supplying some service like free education. There are many people of this view. They are usually socialist (but don't get carried away with this glib categorisation). It is nearly always preferred by those who are going to get something for nothing while others pay. The other main proponents are idealists needing a cause.

Let's move on to more subtle means of 'Learned Helplessness'

The Ombudsman. Is he there for the individual's benefit? Well that is the government's Prima Facie presentation. When looking at the faults in how large organisations work (e.g. government departments), research has shown that the following process takes place:

A search for the guilty
A disruption of the organisation's work
The punishment of the innocent

This process has been translated into the management phrase 'Bring me the head of the Mail Boy'

If you complain about misconduct in your Local Council, first, you have to address that complaint in writing to the source of the trouble. Then the person's superior. Then to the council's complaint department. By the time you have done this your problem has escalated a hundred fold with additional arguments, bogus facts, and perhaps a string of other data. You now have an escalated problem; you are angrier and probably fatigued. You push on and submit to the ombudsman's office. You now have a mass of paperwork and your representations include a large chronology of events created by the complaint process. Providing you have a high level of literacy, otherwise you are screwed, your presentation will be read and judged without comprehension and it will just be dismissed with a few platitudes. The judgement may even be in your favour. "Yes, misconduct was committed. Unfortunately, there is nothing we can do about it. The power lies with the council".

The council gets the Ombudsman's decision and then the recommendation is passed on "this misconduct must not be indulged in again" says the council chief. That is the end of it, except that the council is obliged to publish the figures in relation to complaints and the number of ombudsman's decisions against the council. Only they lie about these figures; nothing happens as was my experience with the London Borough of Redbridge. So you did all that and got nowhere, and they even lied about your complaints as a statistic. You could of course, pay for a

Judicial Review at the High Court, and if you win they can order that the correct statistic is published. You may even get 2/3 of your costs back. Yes, you have made a rod for your own back.

I think you get it 'Learned Helplessness'.

Party Politics

It is natural for people to form themselves into groups of self-interest. The larger the groups get, the more powerful the area of common ground or interest becomes, and the more irrelevant the other interest of an individual or sub-groups become. From this, it is easy to see how parts of an individual can be destroyed in the interest of the greater common good. Groups can be made up of multiple sub-groups but have main aims that are in conflict with other groups. This is obvious as we look about amongst our political parties or religious groups etc. We can theorise as well as see it in the political instance when one party gains power it dominates with its policies and practices at the expenses of those (millions of people) that lost the election.

Here we see the problem of party politics: the tyranny of the majority against the minority. It should be obvious that this cannot be good.

It gets worse when it comes to 99% of the community wanting one thing and the other 1% wanting something else. The 1% just become or are seen as collateral damage. Here in particular we get the tyranny of the many against the few.

This of course is not a new idea and when Britain's Political System was forming, political philosophers such as J.S. Mill[4] claimed that the reason Real Democracy was no good was because mass voting always produced the tyranny of the many against the few. This was one of his main reasons for representative government.

One of his other main reasons was that the populace was too stupid to run a country. If alive today, he would be eating his words. The representative government currently in place is failing to protect the few, along with anyone else that's inconvenient to their management, or, rather, lack of it. Who were the stupid people that got us into this national debt crisis at the moment? Was it the people or the politicians?

No political system can be perfect, but if it is recognised what shortcomings a system has, then compensating elements can be implemented. Democracy requires this. The extended ancient Greek democracy contained idiosyncrasies to fit the culture of the time and any current Real Democracy must be formed in relation to the current culture with a view to the future.

---

4   See 'On Liberty'

This is not a treatise on what the proposed idiosyncrasies of a current democracy should be. This book is making the case that there must be a democracy so as to prevent tyrannies and that there are two essential principles that it must contain to fulfil that aim:-

1. Power must be in the immediate hands of the people as it votes on all and any issues it sees fit.
2. Accountability of anyone in a position of authority, with the power in the hands of the people for their immediate dismissal and/or punishment.

One point worth noting here is that solutions should be designed to see all parties benefit. This is the 'artist vs. pragmatist' argument. The pragmatist thinks the artist is bananas when he makes huge efforts to produce a tiny canvas of weird shapes. But as any applied designer, such as an Architect, knows, an ideal solution can be found at little or no extra cost. It is the pragmatist who sets up limited choices because of his limited thinking and ends up settling on a poor solution, often justified by being 'economic'. The country and the Civil Service are ruled by too many left brains beings. The solution should not be worked on a bartering system of what is best and the rest not bothered with. The bartering practice is the one in use today. In its academic form, this practice is known as 'Cost Benefit Analysis', but it takes all sort of guises.

In government administration, it often takes on the catch phrase 'Is it convenient for us?', otherwise it's collateral damage.

We need a humanitarian design approach which should not be confused with idealism. However, this is a great deal more work than using Cost Benefit Analysis.

In this chapter, I have come away from the main point of this book 'that we do not have democracy', so as to put things into context and give a taste of what setting up a Real Democracy today might entail.

Justice

Humans have a strong sense of Justice. We easily become outraged when we feel someone has wronged us. This indicates that it is an instinct; in other words, we are already pre-programmed with it. What is right and wrong when analyzed seems very variable, and attempts to conclude laws by general principles has never attained universal assent for long. Of course, this is true of all philosophy and may be more indicative of the nature of the intellect than of morality.

Let's look at morality as a flexible system, like our pre-programming of language[5]. We all have the capacity of language from birth and, at around 1 year old, we start speaking no matter what the actual language. Our language capacity develops over time to have similar grammatical components and syntax whatever the language. If the moral instinct is similar, then we may find our moral codes, from one person to the next, are similar in essence.

The natural instinct, however, is over-run by a very artificial society, which is becoming more and

---

[5]   Noam Chomsky, 'Language & Mind'

more dominant. To deal with this we need artificial rules. Conscience is no longer enough. Man made laws have become the order of the day. Alas, they are all too often made to suit an interest group. How can we determine the laws fit the society? It is not that difficult if you let people vote on the proposed law.

Let's take a look at what we mean by Justice. I am going to take a principle and use it as a landmark. It is not absolute but it can be useful.

'Justice is the compensation of a wrong to put the matter right'

Why is this correct? Because I think you could not put forward a fairer proposition. It does, however, have obvious shortcomings. Could Hitler and his few henchmen put right the holocaust, the tortures, and the deaths? No, it is not a practical possibility.

Is it possible to replace a loved one once killed/ murdered? Most people would answer no. London Underground differs, however. They think a human life is worth £1,000,000[6] so provided you don't kill more than 3 people a year it is OK to run the tubes without guards, which costs about 3 million pounds a year.

---

[6]   This figure is somewhat dated now

Psychopaths passing themselves off as Actuaries come up with this kind of thing.

In the British Justice System, how often is a person compensated for the wrong against them?

The answer is NEVER. In the best case scenario you will be awarded all the money you are owed, and this only if you made a special agreement with your solicitor that the costs they receive are equal to the costs awarded against the other side. You will still be out the full costs of the time you expended as well as the heartache and nervous strain, which is usually considerable. So full Justice has not been done. It is a lot worse than what you see. There is the other losing side as they are now paying for the fitted carpets, and a whole lot more, of the solicitor you employed.

You may consider this just punishment of the losing side, but most cases that go to the civil court are on the borderline and both parties believe they are going to win. The decisions are often on a nuance e.g. the interpreted definition of a word.

In Criminal Law, it is far worse. It never considers our principle of Justice. The entire system is based on revenge and discouraging offences.

I will conclude this chapter with the statement that a High Court Judge, Mr Justice Sedley said to me at the end of a case:

"When you come here, it does not matter how good you think your case is, it is a gamble".

Or

English Justice is a roulette wheel on which more than 50% of the numbers are zero and the legal profession are the croupiers.

Justice System

We have touched on Tyranny in respect of politics and politicians. The other major tyranny has its subject and group in the Legal System and the Judiciary.

The politicians, with the backing of the legislature, instead of the people, decide the process, the laws, and the form the legal system takes, the framework and of how those laws are applied and ruled. The Judiciary then makes determinations on those applications and rules.

The police are an adjunct to the system in, bringing criminal violators before the system.

For those that do not yet know, the British Legal System is split into two: 'criminal' and 'civil'. Without going into detail, criminal cases are nearly always brought by the police and civil cases by a private party. Hearings are usually held in either civil courts or criminal courts. Civil cases generally have a financial outcome, but it may be a restraining order or other obligations on a party. Criminal judgements are usually a fine and/or imprisonment and a criminal record held by the state, but it may be also an obligation such as community work. Both have their nuances of process and administration.

These two parts of the legal system constitute nearly all of it. There are, however, three other minor parts. You have probably guessed them already.

1. Government abuses, normally handled by the High Court under a Judicial Review.

    a. The entire legal profession actually work for the Court, and are under its jurisdiction, even if their entire pay is from a private firm or their own clients. So if a member of the legal profession bucks the system, the Judiciary can debar then from practising.
    b. Solicitors Bills. If you disagree with them, then it is you who have to take action against them. That is the complete reverse of the way it works for the rest of society. More of this later.

2. The Judiciary are completely exempt from punishment in their work capacity i.e when sitting in judgement of a case. For example, if an accused citizen steals a Mars bar, the Judge can sentence that person to death. Whilst in practice, the sentence will never happen, at present the Judge is nevertheless exempt from any punishment for bringing in such a judgement.

Let's move on now to

Legal monopoly

The system gets more complicated as you go into it. This is, of course, exactly what the legal profession wants. As it becomes more monopolistic, it creates far more work for the profession and thus gives it greater income. The more the demand, the greater the cost of the supply.

You will be blinded by science

The more mass and complication there is in the laws and the Legal System, the more lost the citizen is, and the more easily duped. The more the mass of rules and data, the more the possible arguments there are. Great for the legal profession—that is the need for their expertise.

The Laws: A Money Making Machine

Whatever the good intentions of the law makers and the lawyers, they have only ever achieved injustice.

The road to hell is often paved with good intentions. If you get involved with the legal system, either by choice or force, you are on the road to hell. Just ask someone who has done it—even if they won. You will, on sufficient questioning, find that they lost something significant.

This has come about because the lawyers, with the Judiciary as well as the Legislature, have made sure that they get well treated and well paid. In short, they have engineered the system for their benefit. It is covered with clever arguments and rhetoric. If you are a monopoly as they are, this is easy.

I have been told by Judges: "When you are here in court what you do is for my convenience"[7], which

---

[7]   District Judge Mendel

was also another way of saying court time is being extended as are the solicitors' bills, which you are going to be paying for. In other words, "my convenience is your expense".

It is when in Civil Law, you have a solicitor's bill assessed (which used to be called 'Taxing the Bill'), that you discover the real inequalities of the legal system. Most people are so exhausted from the court case that they just pay up and rarely challenge the solicitor's bill. Thus ignorance of the Tyranny continues.

Taxation (now called "Assessing the Bill") used to be carried out by a 'Tax Master', usually an ex solicitor (detect any bias?), who then determines what on the solicitor's bill is chargeable and how much that should be. If a photocopying in a shop is 5p, then a solicitor is allowed 50p. That is not much difference is it? Well I make it about a 1,000% difference. I mentioned already that you have to take action against the solicitor if you don't like his bill. If you don't start the proceedings, then he can take you to court and you have lost by default. You cannot now make a defence. Your opportunity has passed. If you do start proceedings, don't forget that you must get at least a 20% reduction on the bill, otherwise you must pay the solicitor's legal costs for the assessment hearing etc. Oops you reduced the bill by 19%. You are considered to have lost the case, and now have to pay a further £1,000 costs to the solicitor and, if you employed a solicitor to make your case, his fee as well. Do you detect anything one sided?

According to 'Cook on Cost', the main book for assessing solicitors costs, a charge in the overhead for the firm's fitted carpets is quite acceptable. Then you could be paying in those overheads for Personal Assistants, the cost of training a new legal recruit or anything normal to the running and practice of the firm such as repairing their bog. Don't forget the gold leaf name on the door. If they have sent a 'With Compliments' slip with a copy of a letter you have already received, that slip has cost you, say, £15, plus copy charges, of course, and postage and miscellaneous. Don't forget the 2 hour interview you had asking for a chronology of events that you might already have already supplied them with. That is just another £300 plus VAT @ 20%. Don't forget the VAT, because establishing the law is a luxury, not a right, so VAT is chargeable.

So you are in a civil dispute with a landlord and an agreement is not possible. You and your legal team believe the word repair means one thing and your landlord and his legal team believe it means something else. Your solicitor eggs on your sense of injustice and you go to Court. You spend 2 days establishing the facts of the case and arguing trivia, but the main issue: 'what the hell does this word repair mean?' is still a mystery. The judge does not like your barrister so decides that the meaning of repair is your adversary's proposition. The Judge has at least 100 precedent cases affirming their definition. He has also got 100 precedents confirming your definition. The Judge can't be wrong, and if he decides in favour of the other side and your solicitor's bill comes to £10,000 as does your opponent's, you now have to pay both. Well, it may well be that your opponent's bill will be taxed down, so he has to pay 1/3 of it.

To sum up: Because the law was inadequate in defining the word 'repair', you get dragged through a misery and had to pay for the pleasure the sum of £17,000. Your consolation statement from your solicitors is "I think you were in the right. The Judge made an error . . . . Do you want to appeal?"

Your opponent is so jubilant in the assertion of his egoism that he feels he has not really lost the £3,000 he did not recover in costs, and forgets about it along with the miserable journey.

Oops you got screwed. Will you learn your lesson? No, you will do it again. Why? Because you are so programmed to believe in the integrity of the legal system that you cannot see the writing on the wall. The LEGAL SYSTEM IS CORRUPT. You, like most people, will still believe in the integrity of the legal system.

Will the Judiciary be bothered on reading this? No, they will be chuckling to themselves at the mastery of the con and the fulfilment of their lust for power.

Not only that, but dispiriting people from engaging in court action is what they want at present, as the courts are massively over inundated.

What you need to be doing is petitioning for Judicial Accountability and reform of the legal system to serve the public and Justice. Petitioning for a system that does not set up the Legal profession to give you a kicking and get rich out of it.

Stop Press

A preliminary bill to impose on solicitors a fixed fee charge on clients is on the table. Is this for your benefit? Is a thousand years of engineering the benefits of the legal profession to be reversed? No it is not. It is so that solicitors can engineer agreements out of court and still get the same, or even more, money than if they went to court. Also, the pressure on the courts for hearing times is reduced. The controversy over costs is lost as the bill is predetermined. You may be saved a taxation but your bill, on average, will be elevated. Are you surprised?

Judicial Misconduct

Whilst history portrays one misconduct after the other, the Judiciary claim purity i.e. zero misconduct. Let's take a historical look.

Take the case of a man in medieval times who was brought before the Feudal Lord on a hanging offence. The Judge/Lord found him guilty and the hanging was duly dispatched. In the evening, the Lord and his guests discussed over dinner if he really was guilty.

Let's come forward to the renaissance. There was Francis Bacon, the man credited with founding the Scientific method and establishing the importance of 'Inductive' and 'deductive reasoning'. He was, at the time, Lord Chancellor: the No1 Judge (all Judges still have a judicial number in ascending importance). In his capacity as Judge in a case, he decided that the bribe from one side was not enough and so he took a bribe from the other side as well. Each party found out about the other's bribe and complained. Queen Elizabeth I found out and sacked him. He was not charged with anything, however, but the loss of his in excess of £1,000,000 per annum salary must have hit him a bit. Well, the monarchy managed to sack a judge. They have done better than any parliament since.

Let's move forward in time to the case of the famous Quaker William Penn (his picture is on the Quaker Oat cereal box), who was the founder of the American State of Pennsylvania.

Whilst still in England, he was accused of something and put on trial. At the end of the trial the Judge directed the Jury to find him guilty. However, the Jury found him innocent, so the Judge put the Jury into prison.

Whilst I was attending a weekend course on Cromwell, I happened to be sitting next to an Oxford University Professor of Law at dinner. I put it to him that the Judiciary does not have a good reputation in respect of misconduct and quoted the above example "Ho, Ho, yes that one" was the response. At least my sauté potatoes did not choke me due to my lack of etiquette.

If this all seems to be becoming a bit farcical like the film 'Dr. Strangelove', when the Atom bomb button is about to be pressed and all you can hear is laughter, don't worry. You'll soon be arrested and imprisoned as a suspected terrorist, extradited to America, have a confession made against you and you'll be put in the electric chair. Your misery will soon be over.

In Georgian times, it really was horrific. In London, there were large numbers of orphans living on the streets. Minor thefts were in abundance. There were a large number of arrests and the Judiciary reacted. Many children were sentenced to life imprisonment or deportation to Australia for stealing nothing more than a comb. The old Bailey was a bastion of oppression, or saviour of combs, depending on which end of the stick you were holding.

Let's come to the near present and look at the research that the reporter Mark Easton put together in his Channel 4 Despatches programme about 10 years ago, 'A report on current English Judiciary in Criminal Law'. The figures and facts below all relate to Mr. Easton's report at this time.

Rape trials are a repugnant thing in themselves, forcing the victim to relive the pain and trauma in a public trial in all its detail over an extended period of time.

The main output of a Judge in a criminal trial is in the summing up at the end of a trial, so it is not a procedure a judge can overlook. However, Judge Robert Brown, in a rape trial, did not give his summing up. This permitted the defence to submit an appeal and drag the trial out for a third time over another 3 years.

How about his Honour Judge Stanley Spence, who gave a headmaster, found guilty of sexually abusing students, a £150 fine and community service? The children remain psychologically disturbed for the rest of their lives.

Or how about Judge Gabriel Hutton who freed guilty Class A drug dealers but gave a 76 year old lady who unwittingly handled drugs, 9 months in prison? This judge had, at the time of Mark Easton report, 37 of his judgements overturned on appeal.

How about Appeal Judge Peter Cox who had 38 interventions on his Crown Court judgements?

Then there is Judge Enrose, who has been reprimanded 38 times by the Appeal Court. He carries on with his harsh sentencing regardless.

Let us not forget Judge David Owen, with 58 overturns of his Judgements on Appeal. Comments from the appeal judges included: "inappropriate, inadequate, irrelevant, dangerous, inaccurate and incomplete. But tra la la la la he is still sitting in Court.

And yet no Crown Court Judge has ever been dismissed for incompetence.

Do Civil Judges fair any better? Answer: No. Many Judges do both Civil and Criminal cases. It does not exactly inspire you with confidence in their specialisation. What do they care, it is only your life savings or future well being.

I once had a case where my car insurance company and the other driver's insurance company could not agree on an accident. There was an arbitration hearing to see if the collision from a parked car that pulled out and tried to do a U turn as I was driving along caused a collision. The judge found that I was at fault. The barrister handling my case was outraged at the verdict and commented: "he was a rogue Judge". I decided to appeal on the basis of misconduct and represent myself. Stupid, you say. You are correct. Whilst we were waiting to be called into the hearing, the barrister from the other side handed me a precedent case. Here there were 3 applicants who appealed a Judgement for misconduct because the Judge was asleep and snoring for most of the case. The appeal judge claimed the original judge was not asleep and just had his eyes closed and was making heavy breathing noises. Are you are wondering what happened to my appeal? You guessed it already.

Judges can be brilliant in the detail as well. For instance, I was sitting in the capacity of expert witness in front of Judge Pitman of the Central London County Court. I had been reading off information from a stereographic sun path diagram. In his written judgement, his Honour Judge Pitman claimed that the expert "could not be correct because the 17th

December was the middle of the winter". The rest of the world must be wrong when it claims winter does not start until the Solstice about 21st December.

One thing you would expect Judges to be expert on is Court Judgements. Don't bet on it. I once had a High Court Stay on a case in Ilford County Court. The District Judge received the stay order from me and the High Court. What did he do with it? He disregarded it and acted on the case regardless. Could it be that this District Judge Sherate and the solicitors, whose bill I was taxing, are friends? Maybe this was someone else in the Court administration making a mess.

What happened when I complained about the Judge? The office that dealt with the complaint said everything was fine. No surprises there.

The Court process is complex with numerous nuances demanding high standards from the legal profession and applicants. This gives the impression that very refined justice is being delivered. Actually, it is only a very big bill you are getting because the legal profession then has to deal with all these nuances and refinements.

I mentioned earlier a Mr Justice Sedly, who was one of the Judges in a High Court case for taxing (assessing) a solicitor's bill. There were three Judges in all sitting in this case. Normally, as in an industrial tribunal case, there is a Judge who understands the employee's side, one that understands the employer's side and one, the legal expert, who is supposedly neutral. Thus we have a designed hearing to balance the biases. Not so in my taxation case. One Judge represented the tax masters, whose judgement I appealed, one was from the Law Society representing solicitors, and one, Mr Sedly, was supposedly neutral. You have probably spotted it that two of the judges represented the bias of the solicitor. So I had already lost the case before it begun. No quite what the public are allowed to see and believe.

Incompetence, roguery and power lusting. But no Judicial accountability, only a job for life.

Golden Rules of Advocacy

English Legal Trials have the reputation of being conducted in the most refined manner, with no stone left unturned. Judges are highly esteemed for their knowledge. Barristers and all the legal staff of the Court are of high integrity, and Justice will be done as a consequence.

Societies need their myths. And, like Hollywood, the English Legal System has a great facade of myth.

A legal trial, in essence, tries to establish the past reality into the present using mainly words. "An impossible task," you say. Of course it is. To try to reconstruct just one minute part of the relevant past in words is impossible. No reality of that past has been created using words, only a partial verbal story of what the barrister wants to convey. Great play is made with this by barristers, with many an illusion spun.

So why does nearly everybody believe in the reality of a total fallacy? Because you believe in it like you believe in a Hollywood film. The greater the illusion takes you in, the more you applaud the wonder of having been deceived. In a film you snap out of the illusion when the film stops. With your view of the validity of the legal system, the suggestion you have been given of its validity continues.

Now that the barrister has the above stage set, what does he do with it? The first Golden Rule he learns is 'You are not there to establish the truth but to convince the Judge or Jury'.

And so the deception magnifies. Philosophers all know arguments are bottomless. Where there is affirmation there is negation. You can only stop at a certain point and say, "this seems about right". What if you don't accept this and have an argument against it? The legal system is an adversarial one that is based on arguments. If you are a barrister and want that extra money to pay for the completion of your swimming pool, you just open out the argument and increase your time on the case, and of course your fees with it.

There are more of these Golden Rules and the legal profession who present cases must learn them till they are second nature. They do this in and out of trials and it is known as mooting skills. In this way, the illusion that Justice is being done is maintained in trials.

Bear in mind that barristers defend and prosecute with equal verve. I n other words they take an amoral stance on their client. However when the barrister becomes a judge suddenly he is whiter that white and only the pursuit of truth and justice will do. Yeah right.

How is any of this going to differ if the political system differs? It is a good question because it is very difficult stopping the legal profession from putting mooting and the golden rules into practice. The shortcoming of the stage set (words creating the past into the present) cannot be changed.

Personal integrity is key to a functional legal system as well as society in general. However, a critical appraisal of the despicable traits which lead to abuse gives a watchdog his armoury for misconduct. With the recognition of the rogue nature of the legal system, abuse by the Judiciary and lawyers can be curbed by accountability.

Judicial Accountability

Tony Blair and New Labour made it part of their manifesto to bring in Judicial Accountability. "Wow, a real claim towards democracy!" I thought. One day the media announced "Tony Blair goes into talks with the High Court Judges on the issue of their accountability".

At the end of day 1 talks, and in contrast to the fanfare at the beginning of the day, Tony Blair leaves a tiny message for the media stating "Accountability is difficult".

Day 2. More media fanfare at beginning of second day talks. At the end of the Day 2 talks, a message left by Tony Blair: "Judicial Accountability does not look feasible". A couple of weeks later Tony Blair's wife is made a Judge and the issue of Accountability is never heard of again.

There remains no Judicial Accountability.

Complex Systems and the Law

There is a relatively new academic discipline called 'Complex Systems'. It is a study of just that, complex systems. It might be the genetic code of a Genome. It might be a social network, or atomic behaviour. What concern us here are the general rules that have been inferred from this study, and that all complex systems follow. One of these rules or principles is that complex systems are 'flexible', otherwise they fail and the system, which may be a life form or made up of many life forms, is destroyed or significantly debased.

The Laws and Legal System make up a complex system. They are not, however, flexible. They are just the opposite, they are rigid. One law applies to all people, all places, all times and all environments (although there may be small qualifications in particular laws here and there). What this tells us is that our system is anti-life and is going to destroy or debase us and/or itself.

WAKE UP SEE THE WRITING ON THE WALL.

"There are laws that enslave man"
"There are laws that help set them free"

Arthurian Legend

Suggestion

Suggestion is the underlying factor in all the branches of manipulation. It goes under the names of propaganda, advertising, manufacturing consent, persuasion and hypnosis. You find it in subtle guises such as a set of punitive contingencies in an organisation, or on a large scale, as in social engineering schemes.

We normally meet suggestion as linguistic directives but the hypnotic cues can be audible, visual or tactile, and individuals usually have a bias towards one of these.

Because the majority of people are egotistical they think they are beyond all this and have a superior will of control. You are unfortunately just another one of the masses.

Suggestion is very simple and very powerful. Take for example the following statement:

"Do not think of the black cat"

Too late, you have done it! The mind works in certain ways and you have to follow it, just as a pin prick will cause your body to jerk.

Take another example. You walk into a room and your colleague says "Are you alright? You don't look well". You think, "What is he talking about? I am fine." But the thought will bother you probably for the better part of the day.

Take Political Propaganda. A common technique is to only give you part of the story. Let's say that part is rigorously true, as far as it goes. It is only when you get the whole story that you discover that what you have been fed is a gross deception. Your mind acts only on the suggested phrase.

E.g. William Hague announces: "The Russians must stop blocking the Syrian Peace talks treaty".

You then think, "Those Russian bastards are preventing peace and causing mass suffering." You then find out the Russians are blocking this particular treaty because it would allow NATO troops to go in and escalate the problem, and so they don't want that particular clause.

There are endless examples but it is the theme of this book to give just a taste of Democracy and Tyranny. You can look and find many examples for yourself.

If you recognise a suggestion as mass mind control, you are probably now thinking, "Do I want to be a stooge by following it?" You are now entering the world of double think. Can we really live like that? No, it is miserable. So we don't bother. Recognise learned helplessness arising. You can't win. You need an honest and caring political system along with a considerate society. If you allow tyrannical systems, you will be messed with.

Experiment: Try watching an English news channel, and then compare it with others such as Russian TV news and the German news channels. Note their emphasis on certain types of news. The absence of other news will also become apparent. Look also for the sentiment (this is the hidden impulse that brings about your beliefs) behind the news item and cross compare different countries' news channels.

Recommendation: Every year a department of the Sonoma State University (USA) publish a book called 'Censored'. Read at least one of these and see what news items get omitted.

The Crowd

How to control, by suggestion, minds on mass has, not surprisingly, been of interest to politicians, governments, and the military for as long as their own histories.

Hitler was a master of it. By watching film recordings of his mass emotional speeches you can see how he worked people up into a unity of hate, egoism, superiority, and wanting the domination of others. Whilst diabolic, it is very instructive.

Hitler gained his first insights by reading LeBon's book 'The Crowd'. It is not a bad place to start and then from there one can expand one's learning into group minds.

Once you get into group minds, it will become obvious why the Law against 'Inciting people to riot' was brought in. Gradually you will gain insight into how governments use mass mind control. The extent to which they use it is a good measure of how much Tyranny is going on, as well as of the extent that your freedoms are being screwed with.

Power Lust

The trouble with having positions of authority is that it attracts those who want power.

The urge for power in man arises naturally and, often it arises with strong exhilarating feelings because it bestows on the custodian access and the privilege to fulfil his desires. If these are consented to, out of respect, then no one has a problem with it. However, when it takes the form of using people as human candles to illuminate the Colosseum so as to facilitate the night viewing of lions tearing people apart in the arena (as was the case in Ancient Rome), then something has gone seriously wrong.

Taking up positions of authority, leadership, and responsibility is an onerous task. If one is not being paid a large salary to compensate, then why do it? How many people do you see in these positions doing it out of altruism? The odd one or two, perhaps. Is fame enough? No, and that is so because most people in authority are not very much liked.

It is power lust that urges them on when remuneration is in short supply. The power urge finds its fulfilment in pushing people around, and on a large scale in devastating nations. This may or may not bring with it the missing remuneration by force.

What type of individual wants to push people around? It is the person who feels inadequate in some way. The power urge can manifest itself through anybody, but it is easiest in the person who feels inferior. This may also come about by inverted egoism e.g. when someone is knocked off his high horse. The psychologist Alfred Adler has written on this extensively in his works on Individual Psychology and the Will to Power[8].

In short, Power Lust becomes oppressive and power positions become filled by those seeking power. This psychology will work its way through eventually to become oppressive rule.

Here, again, we see why it is so important that the people retain overall power so they can check any adverse effects that come into being through the misuse of authority.

There are attempts in our society to 'Self regulate' e.g. the Law Society will regulate and admonish its own members. Yeah right, pull the other leg—it's got bells on it. There are cases of misconduct that are upheld, but only because it tarnishes the reputation

---

[8]   Albeit mostly in the context of healing.

of other members when no satisfactory excuse is present.

Self regulation is another title for tyranny.

Plato observed this kind of power problem 2,500 years ago. Maybe our advanced society will catch up soon.

Dependency

If you make someone dependent, you have power over them. You can do this by financial hand outs e.g. the dole. But loans are the best. Not only are you constrained by all sorts of contractual conditions, but in the case of a house mortgage, your whole life is subordinated to its repayment. And you have done it with consent.

Your health is dependent on the NHS, your security on the Police, your job on the economy, your water on the health control by the health and safety executive. Whether you can build anything is dependent on the council planning department, etc, etc, etc. Then you are dependent in a myriad of small ways e.g. that the roads are repaired so you can drive your car without the wheels buckling or tyres bursting, that business can transport supplies so that you can buy them; that there are sewers so you are not living in sh*t.

What are you not dependent on? Air is free. Wrong. Pollution control is by the government. The last Labour government wanted to tax your 'view'. They never quite managed that one.

Dependency is almost total. Perhaps your spirit is all that is left to you. Oh, sorry, they have told you that does not exist either. There is only Darwinian Materialism.

Many politicians see government as control. The Law, dependency and suggestion are its major tools. What is so clever about the control is that you are subordinated and made to pay for the privilege i.e. you are made to pay tax. All without your consent, or please tell me when you gave your consent?

Corporations use dependency also. Your desires are their main entrapment. Advertising is the stimulant and contract, their law. See the chapter on Corporatism.

Poodle Blair and Empire

Once upon a time, Great Britain had control of about 25% of the world's land mass and 25% of the world's population. It was called the British Empire. Its origins were in trade, but soon after came private armies to dictate business monopolies and its terms. Then came British government control and state armies, and meddling in all sorts of other countries affairs apart from business. However, by the end of the Second World War, Great Britain and its Empire was a spent force and much in debt.

To finance the debt, America forced Britain to sign an agreement to disband its Empire. America had already started to dominate many countries with its economic and industrial influence. It was now set to build its own empire based on economic pressure and persuasion with an undertone of military threat e.g. we will drop an atomic bomb on you if you don't comply.

America's aim appears to have worked fairly successfully, with coercion rather than blood, although the Cold War had its dodgy moments.

The advent of the Yon Kippur War saw America supplying free armaments to Israel, which continue and are currently worth around US$3bn a year. America's policy has become more aggressive and military conquest is the order of these times. We saw Bush senior bomb Iraq and kill tens of thousands of innocent civilians in Baghdad, all under the guise of restraining the Tyrant Saddam Hussein, who did not have weapons of mass destruction (nor was he likely to ever kill anywhere near so many people in his lifetime). Devastation hit many families in Iraq, most of which were opposed to Saddam Hussein.

A second war against Iraq was planned by President Bush junior with Tony Blair as a sidekick.

This alliance had a problem: they had no justification to go into Iraq to hijack its oil. So they tried to manufacture one. That is, they tried to convince the world that Iraq had weapons of mass destruction. However, the expert envoy sent to discover weapons concluded that there were no weapons of mass destruction in Iraq.

Blair now had the task of obtaining evidence. His first attempt was to get signed confessions that stated the existence of weapons of mass destruction. As there were no legitimate confessions, Tony Blair and Jack Straw tried to get confessions made under torture to be legalised. These bogus confessions could then be tendered as evidence on which to go to war with Iraq.

They succeeded in getting confessions under torture legalised in the High Court but failed to push this through the Supreme Court in our land. You can read an account of this by Craig Murry[9], the former British Ambassador to Uzbekistan, where people were signing confessions under torture every day by the hundred.

Having failed at this, Blair now produced a document claiming the British Secret Service had obtained intelligence of weapons of mass destruction. On this basis, Blair got Parliament's support to declare war as did the Americans. Hundreds of thousands are now dead in Iraq. The country is a mass of rubble and devastation. But the Americans and British do have control of the oil, and America has built a permanent base with which to control operations in Iraq and from there the Middle East. This base, located in Baghdad, is disguised as an embassy. This embassy covers 104 acres.

JOB DONE: ●Control of Iraq's oil ●A permanent US military base ●Collateral damage: a nation in tatters.

Tony Blair now has a million pound per annum contract with an American bank as a consultancy

---

[9] See his book 'Dirty Diplomacy'

fee. Whilst Tony Blair's document on which he went to war with Iraq was found to be a fake, Tony Blair is singing and dancing. His immunity from lying, which he shares with all politicians, sets him free. There is no accountability for lying by politicians. So Blair remains free and in luxury.

It is not just Blair who is Bush's poodle; it is Britain that is subordinate to America. To have Real Democracy in Britain, Britain must be free of America's dominance and control. But looking at the American government for the main control, you may well be looking in the wrong place. More later.

If you have not studied economics, you will need to get a handle on why oil is the major factor in world economics and why Henry Kissinger's statement below is so profound:

"If you control the oil you control Nations"

"If you control the food you control the people"

The second part of the statement is indicative as to why crop genetics are being stormed by those wanting control.

The Power Elite

Who runs Britain? Who runs America? Who runs Europe? Who runs the world?

Are these questions even legitimate ones? If we look at Britain first, the answer that springs to mind is the Government. The Government controls the military, police, civil service, the tax spending councils, regulatory inspectors, and local authorities. It makes the laws and supposedly polices them. At first glance, it controls the main powers and so it seems rational to conclude that the Government is the main power and the Members of Parliament are at the top or are the Elite; that is, they are the power elite in Britain.

But when the Worshipful Master of the Grand Lodge of Freemasonry was phoned by his secretary who asked why he was not at the Temple that night he replied, "I'm sorry, I can't make it—my wife has told me I have to do the washing up".

Who is controlling what is not always obvious.

Who is controlling the food prices, for instance? My supermarket trolley load has doubled in price over the last two years and yet the Government Retail Price Index (RPI) has only increased by a few percent each year. Take the price of a chicken. Two years ago I paid £1.99, and then it made a single jump to £2.99. Now I have difficulty in buying one for less than £4.00, save for the special offers. I shop at a superstore. Are the Government in control? They probably are contributing to the rising prices even whilst praising the supermarket company for creating more jobs. But who needs whom? Does the company need the Government, or does the Government need the company? Clearly it's the latter. The company can use the Government's dependency, but such control must be exercised in the right way e.g. please do not obstruct our run away price increases otherwise our job creation will be dead in the water.

We have already seen from the Poodle Blair chapter that Britain is subordinated to America. This was in relation to foreign policy and action. But to what extent are our lives controlled by the USA? What control do they exercise over the Banking and Financial sector? Are we paying America for the privilege of taking our goods for free? The question is not a printing error.

The answer to this last question is: Yes. America is taking our goods, and that of many other countries' goods around the world, for free. This is how it happens:

We once had a world Gold standard, and all countries had to be able to pay for its imports in gold if asked. This standard was abandoned in 1931. We now have the Dollar standard for commodities worldwide. What this means is, if anyone buys a commodity other than in their own country, that commodity is priced in, and generally paid in, dollars.

Take oil, for example. If it increases in price per barrel, that means more dollars are sought on the world market to pay for that increase. This means two things can happen: the value of the dollar goes up in value against other currencies, which means you can get more goods for the same dollar, or America can print more dollars to supply the demand, which means there are more dollars for America to buy goods with. This money came from a printing press i.e. nowhere. America is obtaining goods for nothing, just as you would if you printed your own money.

This is probably the second greatest con, next to you being told you have democracy.

Let's look at the last but one question: who runs Europe? One wonders. Does anybody know anything much about what is going on in Europe other than the MEPs, who are living it up and indulging their power lust, and then make more rules and regulations restricting us and forcing us to pay more. The European Parliament uses more than 100,000 million Euros per year.

One thing we do know about Europe is that the private banks, IMF and European Central Bank now own Greece, which is the land that gave us Democracy and is now a pool of tears.

Where power cliques operate, there are many areas where governments are manipulated. There are, of course, many areas outside of the control of a country's governments anyway. Corporations and institutions can be major and minor players of control, and we will look at them later.

Task: Look to see if there is a small group of Americans that have the power to control the main powers of America. Is the top 1% of the top 1% of the wealth holders, along with a mix of leaders of bankers, military, politicians, corporate CEOs and heads of institutions such as Universities, forming an elite group of dominance? Are such ideas just Myth?

If such a group is feasible, however, it could not survive under Real Democracy.

War

In the 1960s, the futility of the war in Vietnam became obvious to almost everybody in the USA and Europe. The American propaganda machine was rendered useless and the war came to an end.

Who gained from that war? The financiers, weapons manufacturers and suppliers, and the knock-on businesses to those. Just about everybody else lost, even if only a metaphoric tear was shed.

What of the Second World War? Surely Britain and its allies were forced into a war by Germany and they had to defend themselves? This is the schoolboy version. However, one should question why Germany went to war with such gusto. A significant part of the reason was the fault of Britain and the Allies in oppressing the German people so as to pay for the First World War that they lost. The German people could not get a leader quick enough to release them from their oppressors. That turned out to be Hitler and his psychopaths. Once the war had started, the inevitable requirement for allied defence came into play. The tremendous losses of all those involved is still within living memory. Not so for American industry and American world dominance groups. They gained from the Second World War as they did from the Vietnam War. Their own civilians were collateral damage. Over 50 million died in World War II.

You can see the same theme in the Middle East today, themes of military profit, resources control and their acquisition.

If you have doubts of America's conquesting, and that this is not an ongoing policy, then read the book 'In Search of Enemies' by former CIA Officer John Stockwell. He discusses the American military turning their attention for dominance towards other territories after the Cold War was successful in America's favour. Also, as discussed in a previous chapter 'Poodle Blair', you can see Britain's complicity in the American regime.

Would anyone with an ounce of humanity want these slaughters and devastations caused by war? However, they do. That is why the power to control society and its administration must be with the people. That is Real Democracy.

Is Real Democracy possible? Well, Switzerland has managed it for 150 years. It may well be that they will soon become the target of attack by our tyrannical governments because of their success. Certainly their banking industry has been subject to onslaughts.

Corporatism

The world offers its materials and resources for free. Everything we need is here. With our ingenuity we can make all sorts of wonderful things for our needs and enjoyment. However, everything in the world is now owned or monopolised by someone or some group[10], to the exclusion of others.

Communism believes that everyone is entitled to free and equal access to those resources and Capitalism believes in limited ownership, under an obligation of responsibility for those owning the resources. Communism as idealism seems very attractive in theory, but we have seen it in practice with Lenin murdering millions of people, Stalin murdering even more millions, and Mao Tse Tung exterminating more than both Lenin and Stalin, and Hitler put together. That Communism and Marxism are out of synch with human nature does not really

---

[10] All the land in England is owned by the Crown (government). Any freeholds we have are subject to any government restrictions or orders it cares to make. A short study of land law will expose to what a large extent this is.

require further discussion. Russia is now capitalist, and China, whilst sort of waving a communist flag, is really capitalist under some sort of oligarchy.

Accepting capitalism as free trade is somewhat muted. What concerns us here is the extent to which corporations dictate to the people and to government what they are going to have, how they are to behave and that how government will work on their behalf. Needless to say we would rather they did none of these things.

Let's take a look at Stansted Airport and its Public benefit.

When Stansted Airport was first invented as a concept in the 1960s, Global Warming Theory had not even been conceived. The issues were business expansion and more flights abroad, or better holiday prospects, not forgetting, of course, government taxes. There was a public enquiry on a grand scale and a large report on all the issues with laymen, professional Judges, consumer organisations, technical experts etc involved. They resoundingly decided that Stansted Airport should not be built. Ten years later they just went ahead and built it as if nothing had happened, albeit on the quiet. So much for public enquiries.

The British Airport Authority (BAA) used to be a government Inspectorate making sure the airlines and airports conducted themselves morally/

legally. BAA was then privatised and they became instead the businesses running the airports i.e. they became a corporation. So much for an Independent Inspectorate.

Soon they wanted Stansted Airport to expand. The District Council plus a large and well supported action group opposed it. BAA then employed 14 members of the Labour Party, in power at the time, and most of whom were MPs, to support Stansted expansion and force the planning application through the Planning Appeal process. So much for government for the people. More like MPs lining their pockets against the people.

Let's look at Pilkington Glass. A flagship of British industry for some time, it has a history since the nineteenth century of buying up smaller British glass companies, then eradicating their products and increasing the monopoly of their very limited number of patented glasses. Their motto seems to be, 'you will have what we want you to have because that is the most profitable to us and screw variety'.

Note: Pilkington Group is now a subsidiary of NSG Group (a Japan-based company). It was acquired by NSG Group in February 2006

Let's come closer to the present and look at the advent of Low E glass (glass that reflects heat back into the building) and how the Building Regulations have changed to suit Pilkington's business just nicely, thank you. Many people, certainly the general builder, believe that the Building Regulations are law and they must be followed. They are actually a civil servant's interpretation of the law. In the case of Low E glass the law never changed, but the interpretation—the building regulations—did change. When Pilkington improved the performance of their low E glass, the building regulation performance requirement changed shortly afterwards. Was this continual coincidence, backhanders to civil servants, or a policy to improve insulation values? Or persuasion by the business and technical people in Pilkington that the market and the industry needed it? Or was the key issue Pilkington's profits?

Who did not benefit was the builder or glazier who might have priced on the previous glass that he knew was required and now had to supply low E glass that was twice the price at his own expense.

The extra cost is eventually paid by the householder or client whose fuel consumption on heating never changed[11].

The technical and business departments in corporations are always greater than their civil servant counterparts. They can always either outsmart them or coerce them. Notwithstanding, they may

---

[11]   RIBA *Double Glazing Survey* 2000

be setting the Agenda from the beginning of a new Act or Regulation. Sometimes the civil service catch up on the research and you find a company being prosecuted by the State. This seems to be common in the pharmaceutical industry.

The new Localism Act 2011 favours development over protection for the individual or community. Funny that many Conservative financial backers are Building Developers.

With a system of Party Politics, corporations or institutions have to be paid off in kind for the original financial backing and continued support of the respective political party. The populace must have the power to prevent corporate control. Real Democracy is required. The people must be able to vote on all the main issues and laws where accountability can be implemented at the drop of a hat, along with the prevention of adverse developments and policies.

Mad Madness

The extent of the authoritarian abuses, the mind manipulation and the usurping of freedoms going on everyday is enough to drive you mad. It certainly is not helping our mental health, and, along with it, our physical health. Stress can lead to physical illness as well as psychopathologies.

Reports in the media about the shortfall of the NHS with regard to your bodily ills hit the news regularly. But what of our mental health? You occasionally hear of someone who has escaped from a secure mental hospital who then commits a crime, or similarly someone officially released who then commits a crime. What happens if you visit your doctor with a mental problem? Unless he thinks it is serious and warrants a psychiatrist, he will subscribe a drug. From his 15 minutes consultation, it is fair to say he will have next to no insight into your mental state. He will probably cue in on information you give him like if you feel depressed, and on that basis he will probably subscribe something like Prozac with the usual "if it does not clear up in a few weeks, come back".

This does nothing for the cause of the mental problem, and if it does clear up it will probably re-emerge at a later date. You are not referred to a therapist as this is extremely expensive. With 30%[12] of the populace in Britain suffering a psychopathology once a year, there would be a third of the population having therapy, an impossible financial demand. It might solve the unemployment problem, though, with so many therapists about.

So mental health gets pushed under the carpet. God forbid that feeding people with drugs is seen by politicians as a means of easy people control, or that people struggling with mental problems are so self absorbed, that they cannot agitate the state.

Let's take a look at a short history of what goes on behind the scenes.

Mental institutions going back to places like Bedlam have a notorious reputation of doing little to cure patients. Let's start with the Lobotomies, which took place around 1950. By inserting an ice pick via the eye socket and stabbing the frontal lobe of the brain, they found people complained less about certain mental problems. That they were zombiefied might be a better description. Before

---

[12]   Figures by the charity Mind.

the zombification realisation set in, they carried out 18,000 operations[13].

Troubled soldiers coming back from World War II were often diagnosed with PTSD (Post Traumatic Stress Disorder). It was found that if they were re-traumatised then it was possible for them to find release from their psychological problems. It was found that by giving them electric shocks which were sufficiently strong, that soldiers could be re-traumatised, which could then lead to the same cure. Once the electrical equipment was installed in the hospital, more uses were found for it.

One patient, who voluntarily committed himself to hospital due to family and work related stress leading to anxiety, found that when two psychiatrists diagnosed him and prescribed the same treatment, he could not refuse the treatment. Two psychiatrists can override an individual's will. So they wired him up and burnt out a part of his brain so that now the number 9 does not exist for him. All other numbers are OK and his verbal skills are fine. But without the number 9 he is useless mathematically.

Drugs are the main physical tool for mental health today, so let's look at some facts and figures. Pharmaceutical companies are often international. They are some of the largest, as well as financially

---

[13]   Madness by Roy Porter

most powerful, companies in the world. We are into the realm of Corporatism again. The following figures are taken from America, as it represents the largest pharmaceutical market:

The psychiatric drug industry is worth about 1/3 trillion dollars in receipts each year.

The psychiatric profession takes about US$160bn a year

Every 75 seconds a person is admitted to a psychiatric hospital

The American Psychiatric Association produce a book call DSM (Diagnostic and Statistical Manual) of Mental Disorders. There are no statistics in it and this shows the deceptive nature in which it was compiled. It list 374 mental illnesses of which everybody in society can claim at least one. These disorders are not discovered but classified by members voting on their existence. Each year the list increases and a new drug found to sell against the disorder. Market consultants call this 'creating and expanding your market'. Lawyers similarly increase their market every time there is a new Law made.

About 60% of the committee of the American Psychiatric Association (APA) are on the payroll of a pharmaceutical company. Hypothetically, imagine you, as a committee member of the APA, create a new mental illness, say 'Road Rage', and then invent a tranquiliser for it. The pharmaceutical company, whose payroll you are on, are going to reward you handsomely if you manage to get the committee to vote it as a mental illness.

In American schools in 1987, ½ million children were diagnosed with Attention deficit hyperactivity disorder (ADHD). In 1997, 4 million were diagnosed with ADHD. In 2001, 6 million were diagnosed with ADHD. Are all of these kids really mentally flawed? They all, of course, need drugs according to the diagnostics. Or is it that the psychos are the pharmaceutical companies with obsession for profit? I Plump for the latter.

Bear in mind that the earlier DSMs had homosexuality listed as a clinically based mental disorder. Now, by popular demand, it isn't, and is nowhere to be seen as a mental disorder, let alone a clinically mental disorder. We are being made ill in theory then drugged in practice.

Let's move on to psychiatry and its crossover with politics.

"Psychiatry is Politics"
"Politics is Psychiatry"
How much truth is there in this statement?

Certainly, in Communist Russia they held that if you did not agree with the politics then you were mad and were treated accordingly i.e. drugged, electrically shocked, etc.

China, to my knowledge, was not so sophisticated—the government just killed the dissident.

Hitler and the psychiatry of Mengele and the 'SS' give a good insight into psychiatry and politics.

Let's move into the present and take a look at the main APA book, the DSM, and ask how many are political based illnesses e.g. crime, the breaking of a political law and how many are social disparities classed as illnesses e.g. stealing because you are hungry. We find these two categories are a large proportion of the number of mental illnesses listed in the DSM book. None of them are due to actual brain or neurological damage.

Regulations

Regulations are derived from the law but are not themselves law. However, if you infringe a regulation and cannot argue its failure—which, in practise, means you must show that it is somehow false—then prosecution and a sentence will be your lot. Even if you can prove it to the authority concerned, they may well prosecute you regardless, especially in the case of parking tickets and their like.

Regulations are often put forward as enabling and facilitating good practice. But mainly they are restrictions, and they are a massive magnification of the Act of Law (Statutory Instrument) on which they are based. Take the Building Regulations. The Statutory Instrument (Law) on which they are based covers about 4 sides of A4 paper. The associated Regulations take up the shelf space of about 1-2 volumes of the Encyclopaedia Britannica. Professionals often love an increase in the regulations because it will increase their work market, although it is often viewed as another burden by the general employee. What does inevitably happen is that the extra cost of the work put on a company or professional is passed on eventually to the consumer. Any challenge to a Regulation not only requires a lawyer but an expert witness, or even several experts, in the area concerned. That is pretty well doubling your legal bill. In the case of the building regulations, if you are a house owner and you disagree with your local council surveyor and want to challenge their claim, you will find that you have to pay about £500 for a determination to be processed by The Department for Environment, Food and Rural Affairs (Defra). You will not get the money back even if you are right.

What about Parking Regulations? These are really disguised taxation, only they are a subversive means of taxation. They set you up as if you are a criminal offender and then steal your money, in ever increasing amounts if you resist.

Many of the Parking restrictions are beneficial to sections of the community. This is their legitimate face, which makes it possible for them to gain people's acceptance and allow the government to continue to implement the system. But many parking places are just a means of raising money e.g. parking payments for roadside parking. At some point somebody realised that the fines were making a lot more money than the parking meter payments. Thus, it was realised that creating situations whereby drivers break the rules, would raise a lot more money. So arose the '3 minute allowance' past your parking payment time and then a large fine is payable. Later arose the deceptive signage in parking bays where the appearance of a 'pay at meter' sign looks just like a 'Residents Parking Only' sign. For instance, there may be a sign in your bay where one quarter of it is a 'P' on a blue background meaning parking for all, then opposite, on another quarter of the plate, a contradictory statement, such as 'Resident parking only'. Below the big 'P' are time allocations but the numbers partly extend under the 'Residents only' wording. So is it parking for all or parking for residents only? Do the time allocations refer to the 'parking for all' or the 'Residents only'? What does 'Residents' mean? Does it mean residents of England or is it residents of the District you parked in? Or maybe the Residents of the County you are parked in? Is it residents of the street you parked in? You are left to ponder: "what the hell do they want?" Not surprisingly, you get it wrong and you are fined. What happens if you challenge the fine? It costs you incrementally more as it goes along. Can you win? I should coco.

I have described a specific instance but there are many variations to trick you. Generally all 'Parking' signs look like other parking signs, so you automatically are lead to believe they are the same. This is easily done; especially as all other road signs are distinctive. Even the yellow lines at the side of the road do not confuse unlike the parking bay plates. The yellow lines immediately signal the difference between being able to unload or to being able to park at restricted times. In parking bay 'Pay Plates' there are contradictions. This all leads your mind into being deceived. And, of course, this happens time and time again, clocking in large amounts of fines for the governments agents, whilst Jo Smos' (citizen) hard earned money is forced out of him under threat. Consequently his anger and stress levels are added to the 30% psychopathologies that this country's populace sports.

Let's look at one more example in government caring in respect of Social Security and Welfare Payments Regulations. They are a real convoluted set of rules and criteria with loopholes to allow the assessor to do what they want; sometimes to the benefit of the recipient. However, add to that a good number of the fallacies of logic and you end up with criteria such as:

If you own a house, which you purchased, with some extensions on them, you can claim the interest of you mortgage with these extensions included; but if you built the same extension after you bought the house you cannot claim the interest, on the amount borrowed for these extensions, in your mortgage.

Thus the tax payer, that is you several times over, pays for the bureaucracy which persecutes, restricts and abuses your freedoms. As a basic rate taxpayer you have paid for the writing of the regulations and their monitoring. You will further pay for any application in regard to the regulations. Then you will pay again if you have to appeal any oversight that the regulations contain.

So you pay the government, then you pay them, then you pay them again, then some more. What for? To restrict you freedoms, or to simply relieve you of more money.

Too many rules drives people mad. Stealing their money, by subversive means, drives them even madder.

An Ending for a Beginning

The essence of these writings is twofold, that people should hold the power by voting on the main issues and laws and that should be accountability of anyone in a responsible, usually authoritarian, position. These are the keys to preventing tyranny and establishing what society wants, and not what some clique dictates. Consent is a key word in Real Democracy and is nearly always absent in our politics.

We moved on to what tyrannies are currently operating and how they operate. These tyrannies cannot be corrected by a bit of tweaking here and there i.e. by making some new laws or an influx of money to manage a situation. The tyrannies are too fundamental and too opposed to human nature e.g. extreme greed, power lust, or an obsessive desire for luxury. The psychopath or just the clever man with a vice will always adapt and find a way around the law under our system. Only a system with watchmen and tyranny controlled by the masses will prevent this i.e. Real Democracy.

The problems are far more extensive than the examples I have given. I don't doubt that most readers have examples and personal experiences of their own.

Having a workable and beneficial political system is only part of the story. Personal development and integrity of the society's individuals is highly necessary. A society is only as good as the people in it, although, in a successful society, the sum is greater than its parts. Formulating what laws, policies and other adjuncts go with the adoption of Real Democracy is a gigantic task. Then once you have mastered these tasks, you have to confront that no system is perfect. How can this come about when corruption is so entrenched? You tell me your miracle.

Bibliography with Comments

Brooke, Heather 'Your Right to Know' Pluto Press
    The author was the main force behind getting the "Freedom of Information Act" onto the British Government Agenda. The book helps you make use of the Act and its advantages.

Brooke, Heather 'The Silent State' William Heinemann
    The Government's shortfalls and tyrannies, most of it under Tony Blair's Labour Party.

Chomsky, Noam 'Language & Mind'
Cambridge University Press
    Why we are pre-programmed with language.

Chomsky, Noam 'Media Control' Seven Stories Press
    His definition of Democracy is a bit off. Because of this misunderstanding in all strata of society, Real Democracy is impeded. However, he gives some useful insights into political propaganda. A short book.

Cook, Michael J. 'Cook on Costs' Butterworth
    If you challenge a solicitor's bill, this is the reference the professionals use. Despicable.

Dahl, Robert A. 'On Democracy' Yale University Press

Good example of how to turn Democracy into a Roman Republic or Contemporary American Political System. He changes the definition of *'kratos'*, which is 'might/rule', into just 'rule', thereby giving himself licence to go almost anywhere.

Davies, J.K. 'Democracy & Classical Greece' Fontana Press

The background to Democracy and Ancient Greek Society around the time of origin of democracies.

It is not surprising that the simple 'Essence of Democracy': the prevention of Tyranny; the power of the people to directly rule themselves, and accountability of those in authority, has been lost under the mass of historical facts.

Dutton, Kevin 'Flipnosis' William Heinemann

Gives interesting accounts of the Psycopath, Learned Helplessness and Misdirection.

Engdahl, William F. 'Gods of Money' Progressive Press

Mark Twain said "The root of all evil is not having money". It is when those that have power perceive they don't have enough money that the real troubles begin. Worse still is the fear of future security, it is then that the thoughts arise that: We must secure our future abundance by force. Engdahl gives a good account with an alternative view of monetary and power abuse. He has the skill to unearth the facts which for many investigators remain buried.

Hoffer, Eric 'The True Believer' Harper Collins
A classic. Hoffer was a labourer and a dock worker all his life but wrote this book and went on to be awarded the Presidential Medal of Freedom. The book is about the thinking mechanics of revolutions.

Lebon 'The Crowd'
Written from observations made from crowd revolts during the rise of the French Revolution. A book that influenced Hitler, who developed its ideas and used them in his speeches at the mass rallies, etc.

Linder, Wolf 'Swiss Democracy' Palgrave MacMillan
Some insights into a Real Democracy working today.

Machiavelli, Niccolo 'The Prince' Oxford Paperbacks
Written during the Renaissance in Italy. It is probably a re-emergence of the thinking of Ancient Roman Imperialism. It is a short treatise on how to seize political power and retain it. It is divorced from feeling and it is a psychopath's bible to military dictatorship. Compare its ideas with British and American Foreign Policy.

Mills, C. Wright 'The Power Elite'
Oxford University Press
A classic written in the 1950s by an American Sociologist. It explores the why, where, when, who,

what and how of America being controlled by a Power Elite inside and outside government.

Mill, John Stuart 'On Liberty' Penguin
A classic. Mill was an expert Logician. He advocated Representative Government. He thought the populace too stupid to run a country and thus Real Democracy was a mistake. Would he hold that view today?

McGill, Ormong 'The New Encyclopaedia of Stage Hypnotism' The Anglo American Book Company
How to recognise when hypnosis is going on and how to do it. Geared to the somnambulistic state. The suggestion we get in a political and advertising context is unlikely to put you in a trance but the states are related.

Moncrieff, Joanna 'The Myth of the Chemical Cure' Palgrave McMillan
A psychiatrist's account of medically prescribed drugs and the misuse and false claims by the medical and pharmaceutical industry.

Murray, Craig 'Dirty Diplomacy' Scribner
A must read. The author was a former British Ambassador to Uzbekistan. It is autobiographical. He speaks out about the mass tortures and murders and the tyrannies going on in Uzbekistan and the quiet support given to that by the then Labour government under Blair, along with the American government.

(editor) Renston, Stanley A. 'Political Psychology'
Macmillan Press

How many political theorists think today. Help.

Politics, sociology and behavioural psychology are not sciences despite many academics in these areas trying to claim scientific status.

For science to be science, it must be able to be tested again and again and again, and the results obtained be the same or within a small variation of error. For this to be possible the variable elements in an experiment should he kept to an absolute minimum. With organic life this is impossible; with the mind's temperamental variations, the situation is even worse. When you apply this on a national or world scale, the variables are so extensive that all you have is a basket case, let alone a scientific case.

Thus, while research in these areas may be interesting—or even useful—is has more to do with the artful way in which they are handled than the scientific.

Robertson, Geoffrey 'The Justice Game' Vintage Books

Accounts of the tyrannies in the legal system by a Queen's Council Barrister (Q.C.). Describes actual cases and the abuses they suffered, along with the shortfalls of the legal system. A must read if you are unaware of what is going on in the current practice of the legal system.

Russell, Bertrand 'An enquiry into meaning and truth'
Unwin

The idea that 'words are transparencies' is recounted here. Bertrand Russell expended a great intellectual effort to find what in language could be exacting i.e. like mathematics. He admitted failure, much to the chagrin of the political and legal professions.

Saunders, Frances S. 'Who paid the Piper'
Granta Books

Written by an Oxford university graduate, this book is a long haul read with all the details expected of a journalist. It describes how the CIA transferred the centre of the Art Wold from Paris to New York and the large amounts of money thrown at the project to make it work. So much for a free market, or a free anything else.

Pirie, Madson 'How to win every argument' Continuum

Exposition on the use and abuse of logic. Logic is a subject that should be taught to everyone because it is so basic to all thinking. There is clearly something amiss with our education system.

Logic will help remove the mask of political rhetoric.

Sharp, Gene 'From Dictatorship to
Democracy' Profile Books

Apart from the author not advocating Real Democracy, the book formulates how to overthrow a government without violence. Translated into over 30 languages, the book has been the forerunner of numerous armed insurrections. The author is adamant that he has no connections with the CIA; but the author needs no connection, the CIA have just found the book a useful tool. It may, however, end up bringing about their demise.

Stockwell, John 'In Search of Enemies' W.W. Norton
Written by a former CIA Task Force chief, it details how the US deliberately finds new wars to fight.

Volcansek, Mary L. 'Judicial Misconduct'
University Press of Florida
To say trying to find a book on Judicial Misconduct is difficult, is in the ball park of trying to recount how many pink elephants one has seen flying. However, this is one and it looks briefly at American, British, Italian and French cases, or should I say the lack of admission of them by the Judiciary?

Peter Phillips and Project Censored
'Censored 2005' Seven Stories Press
Published every year by Sonoma State University (USA). Significant news stories that should be major news but somehow never get looked at by the mainstream media. Why? Look at the article 'Policy for the New American Century (PNAC)'

Fiction Orwell, George '1984' Penguin
Unheeded, weep.

DVDs
Farenheit 9/11, Michael Moore

Good watch. American government tyranny with British acquiescence.

Psychiatry (An Industry of Death)
The citizens' commission on Human Rights

It is a one sided take, but no less horrific for it. Ask yourself: do you really believe the government is in control with the citizens' best interests at heart?

Hitler: 'Triumph of the Will, part 1, part 2' DemandDVD

How to manipulate a Nation through the crowd. Hitler demonstrates his mastery over the German group mind. The film starts out showing the magnificence of a German city and its German heritage. How wonderful the German people are to have built it and what a treasure it is to live in. Its beauty, charm and security. Then the film extends the association to the people and how important they are. The film pumps up the ego and builds the identification of the individual as part of the nation, along with all the wonder that it is being portrayed as, eventually subordinating the person to the national group whilst actually making the individual a small expendable component.

Does anything seem familiar as a British national? If yes, where did that come from? What are the hidden persuaders? Or were you born with it?

The War You Don't See, John Pilger, Network DVD

A TV news reporter. Shows how reporters and news are manipulated by governments and interested parties Along with other non ethical media practices.